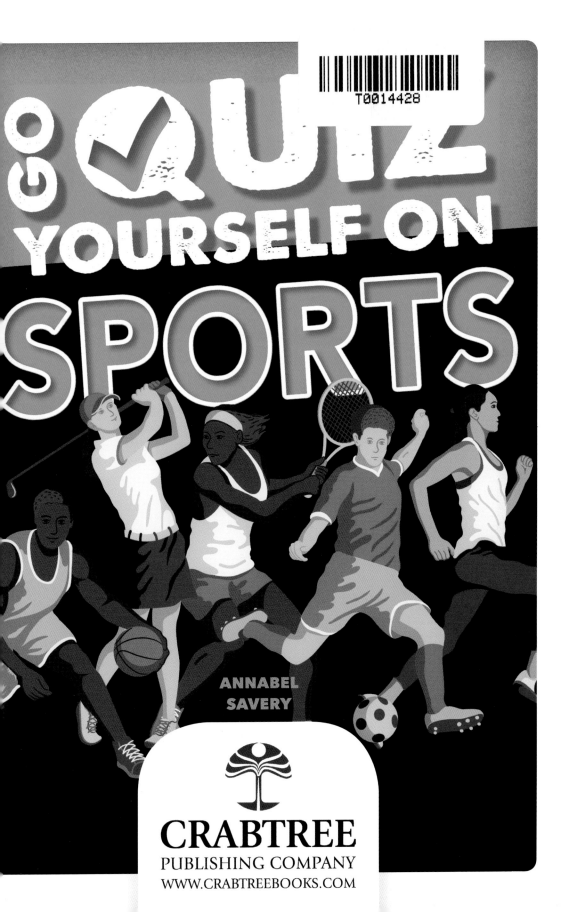

GO QUIZ YOURSELF ON SPORTS

ANNABEL
SAVERY

CRABTREE
PUBLISHING COMPANY
WWW.CRABTREEBOOKS.COM

T0014428

CRABTREE
PUBLISHING COMPANY
WWW.CRABTREEBOOKS.COM

Author: Annabel Savery
Editorial director: Kathy Middleton
Series editor: Izzi Howell
Editor: Crystal Sikkens
Proofreader: Wendy Scavuzzo
Series design: Rocket Design (East Anglia) Ltd
Prepress technician: Katherine Berti
Print coordinator: Katherine Berti

Every effort has been made to clear copyright.
Should there be any inadvertent omission,
please apply to the publisher for rectification.

The website addresses (URLs) included in this book were
valid at the time of going to press. However, it is possible that
contents or addresses may have changed since the publication
of this book. No responsibility for any such changes can be
accepted by either the author or the publisher.

All facts and statistics were correct at the time of press.

Picture acknowledgements: Getty: VasjaKoman 3cbr &
8t & 10bc, 24bc & 28br, pikepicture 24br, Big_Ryan 30b
& 34-35b, FrankRamspott 38b; Shutterstock: Lisa Kolbasa
cover & 1, Macrovector 3tl & 15b, aurielaki 3tr &21bl, Fred
Ho 3ctr & 36-37c & 40b, KittyVector 3cl & 39b & 40 tl tr cr
& 41 cr, Colorcocktail 3bl & 6t, Steinar 3br & 15tr & 17tr,
Hennadii H 4 & 46bc; Chistoprudnaya 4-5b, Mictoon 4-5b,
justone 4-5b, Michal Sanca 6b & 11bl, sahua d 7t & 10br,
Olena Minko 7b & 10bl, artsmith 8b & 10bl, DenisKrivoy 9tr,
Inspiring 9t & 46br, Sentavio 9b, kstudija 12t, tele52 12-13b,
marinat197 13b & 47bl, VectorShow 14l & 16-17b, alphabe
14c, Inspiring 14r & 16-17tl c br, brichuas 15ct, Macrovector
15b, Artreef 18tr & 23 tl & 47br, Artisticco 18cl, Artisticco
18cr, Artreef 18b, Katarzyna Wojtasik 19tr, Macrovector 19b
& 22-23b, Milan Student 20t, aurielaki 20b & 23tl, kontur-vid
21t, aurielaki 21bl & 22tr, aurielaki 21bc & 23cr, aurielaki
21br & 22cr, Krafted 24 tl & 29bl, VAZZEN 25t, Donald
Sawvel 25c, Bakhtiar Zein 25b & 29br, SkyPics Studio 26,
Macrovector 27tl, aurielaki 27tr & 28bl, shopplaywood 27b,
VAZZEN 30t, filip Robert 31t, Inspiring 31b, Pirina 32-33c,
Hennadii H 32-33b, Nigel Kirby Photography 33cr, Lio putra
36t & 41tr & 46bl, Olena Minko 37t & 41bl, Macrovector
37bl, Art of Maria 37br, Vizualbyte 38tl & 41br, MSSA 38tr,
KittyVector 39t, omiksovsky 39c, Paragorn Dangsombroon
42t & 47bc, Professional Bat 42t inset, Anatolir 42c, PenWin
42b, Naddya 43ctl, d'Naya 43ctc, Dzm1try 43ctr, Nadya_Art
43cbl, AnastasiiaM 43cbc, Blan-k 43b. All design elements
from Shutterstock.

Library and Archives Canada Cataloguing in Publication

Title: Go quiz yourself on sports / Annabel Savery.
Other titles: Sports
Names: Savery, Annabel, author.
Description: Series statement: Go quiz yourself |
   Includes index.
Identifiers: Canadiana (print) 20200381679 |
   Canadiana (ebook) 20200381954 |
   ISBN 9781427128751 (hardcover) |
   ISBN 9781427128812 (softcover) |
   ISBN 9781427128874 (HTML)
Subjects: LCSH: Sports–Juvenile literature. | LCSH:
   Sports–Problems, exercises, etc.–Juvenile literature.
Classification: LCC GV705.4 .S28 2021 | DDC j796–dc23

Library of Congress Cataloging-in-Publication Data

Names: Savery, Annabel, author.
Title: Go quiz yourself on sports / Annabel Savery.
Other titles: Sports
Description: New York : Crabtree Publishing Company,
   2021. | Series: Go quiz yourself | Includes bibliographical
   references and index. | Audience: Ages 9-14+ years |
   Audience: Grades 4-6 | Summary: "Read all about different
   sports from around the world-the top competitions, amazing
   moments in sports, and athletes who have wowed the
   world! Then see if you can answer questions, such as:
   How many events are there in the Summer Olympics?
   What are the three skiing disciplines? What happens
   in a speed-climbing race?"-- Provided by publisher.
Identifiers: LCCN 2020046061 (print) |
   LCCN 2020046062 (ebook) |
   ISBN 9781427128751 (Hardcover) |
   ISBN 9781427128812 (Paperback) |
   ISBN 9781427128874 (eBook)
Subjects: LCSH: Sports--Juvenile literature.
Classification: LCC GV705.4 .S36 2021 (print) |
   LCC GV705.4 (ebook) | DDC 796--dc23
LC record available at https://lccn.loc.gov/2020046061
LC ebook record available at https://lccn.loc.gov/2020046062

Crabtree Publishing Company
www.crabtreebooks.com   1-800-387-7650

Published by Crabtree Publishing Company in 2021

First published in Great Britain in 2020 by Wayland
Copyright ©Hodder and Stoughton Limited, 2020

**Published
in Canada
Crabtree Publishing**
616 Welland Ave.
St. Catharines, Ontario
L2M 5V6

**Published in
the United States
Crabtree Publishing**
347 Fifth Ave
Suite 1402-145
New York, NY 10016

Printed in the U.S.A./122020/CG20201014

CONTENTS

HOW TO USE THIS BOOK

This book is packed full of amazing facts and statistics. When you've finished reading a section, test yourself with the questions on the following pages. Check your answers on pages 44–45 and see if you're a quizmaster or if you need to quiz it again! When you've finished, test your friends and family to find out who's the ultimate quiz champion!

BE A SPORT!

From kicking a soccer ball to paddling a surfboard, from skiing downhill to hitting a ball down a tennis court—we love sports! Whether on our own or in a team, watching with a crowd or just out for a jog, we use sports to keep active, healthy, and most of all to have fun!

8,000 sports have been recorded worldwide!

(and yes, that includes camel racing!)

WHO'S WATCHING

Aside from playing sports, millions of us watch sports every day. Soccer is the sport most covered by the media, with cricket and field hockey next in line. Table tennis has a huge fan base in Asia, whereas basketball and football **dominate** the USA's sports media.

SPORTS
TOP
TEN

The most played sports in the world

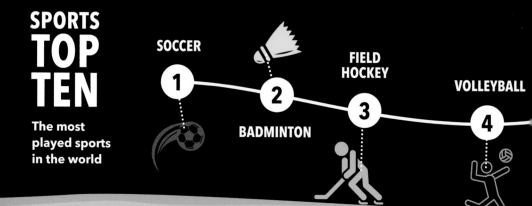

SOCCER 1

BADMINTON 2

FIELD HOCKEY 3

VOLLEYBALL 4

OLD AND NEW

French cave paintings dating back to 3000 BCE show people wrestling. This sport was also part of the ancient Olympics—a contest that took place every four years and was open only to men. New sports are being developed all the time. For example, bossaball combines volleyball, soccer, gymnastics, and capoeira (a Brazilian **martial art**).

Soccer

Diego Maradona, Argentina
Dribbled the ball past seven English players, including the goalkeeper, to score the "Goal of the Century" and win the 1986 World Cup quarter final. Argentina went on to win the World Cup.

Swimming

Michael Phelps, USA
He won eight gold medals at the 2008 Olympics.

Marathon

Eliud Kipchoge, Kenya
Set a new world record at the Berlin **Marathon** in 2018, running it in 2 hours, 1 minute, and 39 seconds.*

GREAT SPORTS MOMENTS

Tennis

Martina Hingis, Switzerland
In 1997, at age 16, she became the youngest tennis player to ever reach world number one!

Swimming

Natalie du Toit, South Africa
Carried the flag for the 2008 Olympic and Paralympic Games. She won five gold Paralympic swimming medals.

Cricket

Brian Lara, Trinidad and Tobago
The West Indies batsman scored 501 "not out" for Warwickshire against Durham in 1994.

Track and Field

Jesse Owens, USA
This African-American athlete won four gold medals at the 1936 Berlin Olympics.

*In 2019, Kipchoge set an even faster time of 1 hour, 59 minutes, and 49 seconds. It was not in an official competition, so it does not count as a new world record.

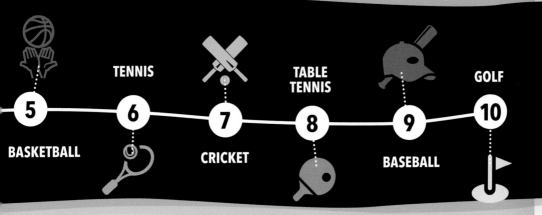

5 BASKETBALL **6** TENNIS **7** CRICKET **8** TABLE TENNIS **9** BASEBALL **10** GOLF

ON THE BALL

Ball sports are some of the most popular in the world. Whether round or oval, hard or full of air, balls are fiercely fought for and used to score points. Good ball skills are key in these sports!

SOCCER

This sport is played in every corner of the world! Soccer players aim to control the ball and score more goals than the other team. Any part of the body can be used to control the ball, except for the hands and forearms. Only the goalie can pick up the ball.

FIFA **2018** WORLD CUP NUMBERS!

6 GOALS
top scorer:
Harry Kane

169
total goals scored

49,651
passes made

485
most passes:
Sergio Ramos

27
most saves:
Thibaut Courtois

19 YEARS, 152 DAYS
youngest player:
Daniel Arzani

16 GOALS
top scoring team: **Belgium**

RUGBY

Could you catch an egg-shaped ball, slippery with mud and rain? Skilled rugby players throw and kick the ball to gain ground and score tries, but they can only pass the ball backward! There are two types of rugby: union and league.

 CAPTAIN'S CAPS   Richie McCaw, New Zealand: **148 caps**, won **131** games, **111** games won as captain

FIELD HOCKEY

Ancient forms of hockey were played in Egypt 4,000 years ago! In the modern game, two teams compete to score goals using a small, hard ball controlled with a hooked stick.

DUTCH RECORDS!

2018 Women's Hockey World Cup, the Netherlands' XI (eleven):

Conceded only **3 goals!**

 Biggest win ever: **12–1** vs. Italy

Tournament total: **35 goals!**

FOOTBALL

Padded-up football players crash into each other as they battle for the oval ball. Teams use a sequence of runs or throws to complete a series of "downs." They have four downs to gain 10 yards (30 feet / 9 m). Players score touchdowns by carrying the ball into the opposing team's end zone.

❄ ICE BOWL

1967 NFL Championship, Green Bay, Wisconsin.
This contest between the Dallas Cowboys and Green Bay Packers for a place at the Super Bowl took place in −13 °F (−25 °C) conditions with the wind chill factor!

COURTSIDE

Speed and accuracy are key to these court sports. They are all played on marked courts either indoors or outside.

NETBALL

Netball players can throw or bounce the ball to each other, but they cannot move with the ball. With just three seconds to pass, they must think fast! Goals are scored by throwing the ball through the 10-foot (3-m)-high net.

 TOP SCORER Mwai Kumwenda from Malawi has scored 300 goals in a single tournament!

BASKETBALL

Famous for their height and athleticism, basketball players also need great ball skills. Dribbling is key to moving the ball quickly down the court. When a team gains possession of the ball, the players have just 24 seconds to attempt a shot!

TALLEST AND SHORTEST

2 M

SUN MINGMING
7 ft 9 in
(2.36 m)

1 M

MUGGSY BOGUES
5 ft 3 in
(1.60 m)

VOLLEYBALL

How about a game of volleyball? Head to the court—or the beach! Teams pop the ball over the net to win rallies and points. After the serve, each team can use up to three hits to send the ball back the other way.

SNOW JOKE!

Snow volleyball is the latest form of this high-power, fast-paced sport.

5 KEY SKILLS

set

spike

serve

dig

dive

TENNIS

Top tennis players face each other across a net and must win a **rally** to win a point. Rallies are won when the opponent can't return the ball, or when the ball goes out of play. Matches can be played as men's and women's singles or doubles, mixed doubles, or wheelchair singles or doubles.

11 HOURS 5 MINUTES

Longest match: Nicolas Mahut and John Isner, Wimbledon 2015

163.7 MPH (263.4 KPH)

Fastest serve: 2012 Sam Groth

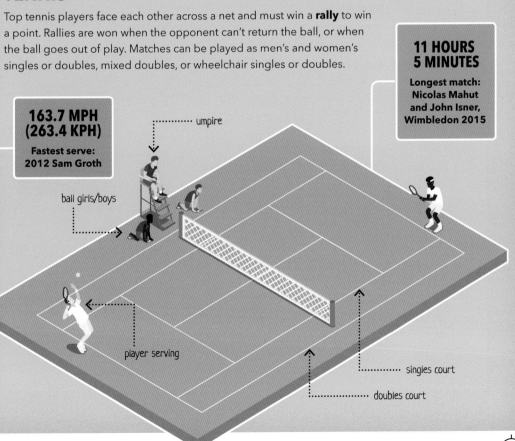

umpire

ball girls/boys

player serving

singles court

doubles court

GO QUIZ YOURSELF!

1. Give three reasons for people to play sports.

2. How many sports have been recorded worldwide?

3. What ancient sport dates back to 3000 BCE?

4. Which sports are combined in bossaball?

5. How many gold medals did Michael Phelps win at the 2008 Olympics?

6. Which body parts can soccer players NOT use to control the ball?

7. How many total goals were scored in the FIFA World Cup 2018?

8. In football, what distance must be gained in four "downs"?

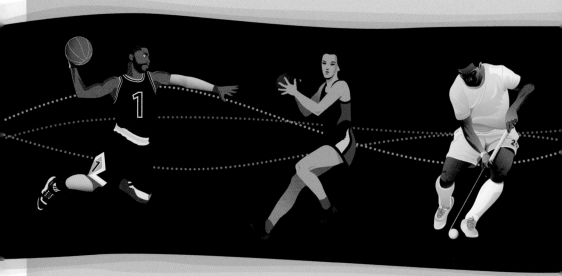

9 How many goals were scored by the Netherlands' XI at the 2018 Women's Hockey World Cup?

10 What are the two different types of rugby called?

11 How many caps has Richie McCaw had?

12 In netball, how many seconds do you have to pass the ball?

13 How long does a basketball team have to score once it has possession of the ball?

14 In volleyball, how many hits can the receiving team make before the ball must be passed back to the other side?

15 What is the latest surface used for volleyball matches?

16 Who holds the record for the longest tennis match?

17 How fast was Sam Groth's 2012 world-record serve?

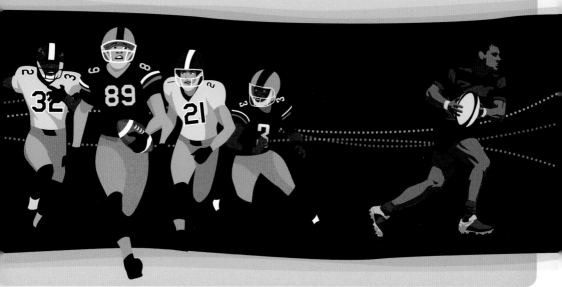

TRACK OR FIELD?

Whether you want to jump, run, or throw, track and field allows athletes to specialize in specific events. There's something for everyone!

RUN AND JUMP!

Track events include sprints and long-distance races. In hurdles and steeplechase, athletes must jump over obstacles as they run down the track. Field events include throws and jumps. The competitor who throws farthest or jumps highest or farthest wins. Throws include hammer, discus, javelin, and shot put. Jumping events include the long jump, triple jump, high jump, and pole vault.

THE STADIUM

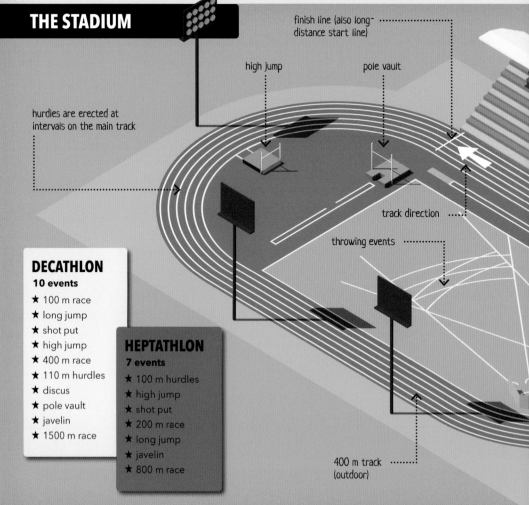

finish line (also long-distance start line)

high jump

pole vault

hurdles are erected at intervals on the main track

track direction

throwing events

400 m track (outdoor)

DECATHLON
10 events

★ 100 m race
★ long jump
★ shot put
★ high jump
★ 400 m race
★ 110 m hurdles
★ discus
★ pole vault
★ javelin
★ 1500 m race

HEPTATHLON
7 events

★ 100 m hurdles
★ high jump
★ shot put
★ 200 m race
★ long jump
★ javelin
★ 800 m race

THE SUMMER OLYMPICS

The Summer Olympics take place every four years.* They last two weeks and include more than 300 events. More than 11,000 athletes from more than 200 countries take part.

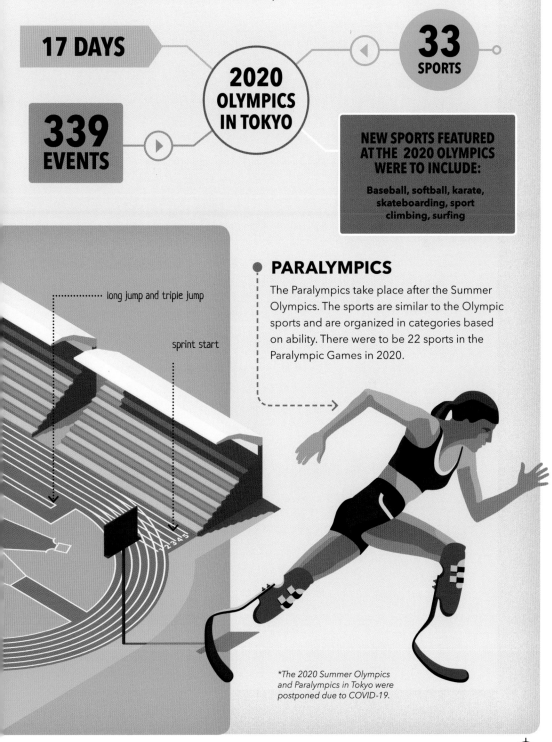

17 DAYS

33 SPORTS

2020 OLYMPICS IN TOKYO

339 EVENTS

NEW SPORTS FEATURED AT THE 2020 OLYMPICS WERE TO INCLUDE:

Baseball, softball, karate, skateboarding, sport climbing, surfing

long jump and triple jump

sprint start

PARALYMPICS

The Paralympics take place after the Summer Olympics. The sports are similar to the Olympic sports and are organized in categories based on ability. There were to be 22 sports in the Paralympic Games in 2020.

*The 2020 Summer Olympics and Paralympics in Tokyo were postponed due to COVID-19.

MAKING A SPLASH

It's fun to have a dip at the local pool or splash in the lake. It takes skill to control a craft on a river or the open ocean. When you have mastered it, it's a thrilling ride!

SWIMMING

Four main strokes can be used to power you through the water: front crawl, backstroke, breaststroke, and butterfly. In **medley** races, the strokes are used one after the other.

DIVING

Divers spring from boards set above the water and perform **somersaults** while in the air. Springboards are bouncy and are 3 feet (1 m) or 10 feet (3 m) high. Platforms are solid and set at heights of 16, 24.5, or 33 feet (5, 7.5, or 10 m). Some competitors dive in synchronized pairs: mirroring each other's movements.

platform level

33 feet (10 m)

Thirty-three-foot (10-m) platforms are used at the Olympics and World Championships. (That's the height of two adult giraffes!)

water level

16 feet (5 m)

Pools with a 33-foot (10-m) platform are 16 feet (5 m) deep.

 TRISCHA ZORN, USA

Trischa was born with aniridia, which causes problems with eyesight. She started swimming at age 10.

★ 5 individual gold medals at her first Paralympics in 1980

★ 5 individual gold medals at 1984 Paralympics

★ 12 gold medals at 1988 Paralympics

SAILING

Sailing divides into fleet, match, and team races in which crews compete over a set course close to shore and longer offshore races. Oceanic races are offshore races over distances of more than 800 miles (1,287 km) of water.

Australia

start/finish

210 DAYS

In 2009–2010, at age 16, Australian Jessica Watson sailed her 30-foot (9-m) yacht *Ella's Pink Lady* 23,000 **nautical miles** (42,596 km), solo, non-stop around the world!

ROWING

Row, row, row your boat! But what kind of boat? In scull boats, rowers have a set of oars each. In sweep boats, each rower has one oar and they row on opposite sides.

SIR STEVE REDGRAVE, GREAT BRITAIN

5 Olympic gold medals, the fifth at age 38

9 World Championship gold medals

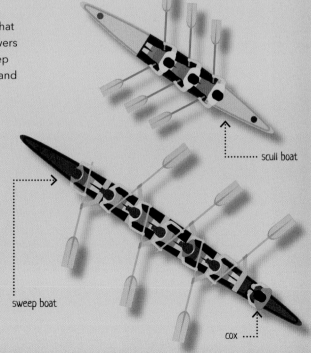

scull boat

sweep boat

cox

GO QUIZ YOURSELF!

18 In track and field, what are the four jumping field events?

19 How many events are there in a decathlon?

20 What type of event is a sprint race?

21 How long is an outdoor running track?

22 How many events are there in the Summer Olympics?

23 Where were the 2020 Olympic Games to be held?

24 How many sports were there to be at the Paralympics in 2020?

25 How many events are there in the heptathlon?

26 Name two of the four main swimming strokes.

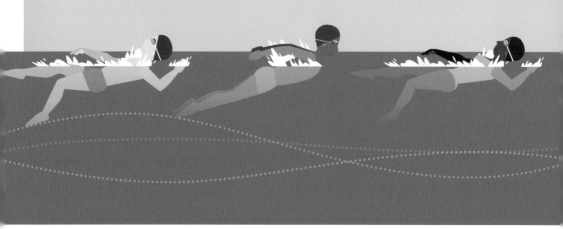

27 How many gold medals did Trischa Zorn win at the 1998 Paralympics?

28 In diving, which is higher: springboards or platforms?

29 How deep are diving pools that have a 33-foot (10-m) platform?

30 What is an oceanic sailing race?

31 How old was Australian Jessica Watson when she sailed solo around the world?

32 How long did Jessica Watson take to complete her around-the-world trip?

33 In a sweep boat, how many oars does each rower have?

34 How many World Championship gold medals does Sir Steve Redgrave have?

ON THE SLOPES

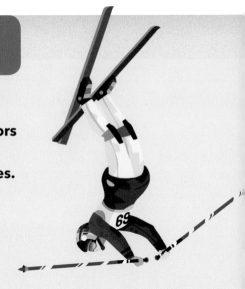

Skiers and snowboarders whoosh down the slopes! Freestyle competitors complete stunning aerial **moves and tricks to the wonder of their audiences.**

SKIING

Skiing is divided into different **disciplines**, such as alpine skiing, cross-country, and ski jumping. Alpine skiers whiz down steep mountains or twisting **slalom** courses. Cross-country competitors race over long distances with steep climbs and descents.

cross-country skier

alpine skier

UP AND AWAY!

Ski-jumping athletes speed down a steep hill and launch into the air from a take-off ramp. They must travel the farthest distance possible before making a controlled landing on the downward slope. **Nordic** combined events include cross-country skiing and ski jumping!

831.7 FEET (253.5 M) World record ski-jump distance recorded by Austrian Stefan Kraft in 2017.

SNOWBOARDING

Slopestyle snowboarding uses a course similar to a skatepark, with rails and jumps. The Big Air event involves sliding down a ramp 161 feet (49 m) high, taking off into the air, and performing tricks, before landing. In snowboard cross, four to six boarders race a course of bumps, rolls, turns, and drops.

CHLOE KIM
USA

5
X Games superpipe wins

5
World Cup halfpipe wins

HALFPIPE

The halfpipe competition is set on a vast U-shaped pipe 22 feet (6.7 m) deep.

Boarders slide down each side, taking off for tricks at the top!

WINTER OLYMPICS

The winter games take place every four years, off-set by two years with the Summer Olympics. The Beijing Winter Olympics in 2022 will feature 109 events in seven winter sports.

WINTER OLYMPIC EVENTS INCLUDE:

FIGURE SKATING

BIATHLON

SPEED SKATING

SNOWBOARD CROSS

SKELETON

CURLING

ICE HOCKEY

BOBSLEIGH

ICE IS NICE

A number of sports take place on slippery ice! Ice hockey, speed skating, and sliding sports are super-fast, while figure skating and curling rely on precision **movements**.

ICE HOCKEY

Fierce ice hockey players use sticks to control and score goals with a hard rubber puck. High skating speeds mean crashes are part of the game, so players are fully padded to avoid injury.

ICE HOCKEY GOALIE

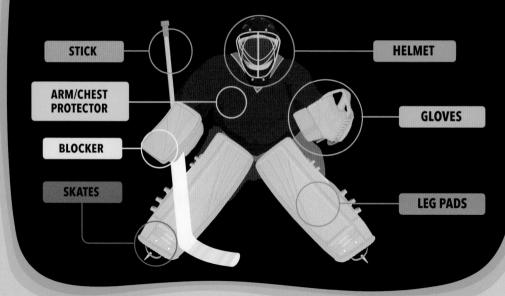

- STICK
- ARM/CHEST PROTECTOR
- BLOCKER
- SKATES
- HELMET
- GLOVES
- LEG PADS

ICE SKATING

Long- and short-track speed skaters race for the fastest times. Figure skaters perform routines to music and are judged on **execution** and accuracy. Athletes can compete individually, in pairs, or in teams.

figure skaters ·······>

1,312 FEET (400 M) The length of a long speed-skating track

CURLING

Curling teams glide polished **granite** stones along a flat ice sheet. The aim is to get the stone as close as possible to the target. You'll see curling players sweeping the ice with brooms to speed the stone along.

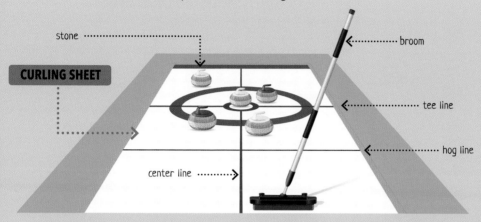

stone

broom

CURLING SHEET

tee line

hog line

center line

8 STONES PER ROUND

10 ROUNDS PER MATCH

SLIDING

Sliding sports take place on narrow, twisting ice tracks that athletes slide down at high speeds. A bobsleigh is an enclosed sled that holds crews of two or four. A monobob is a smaller enclosed sled for solo athletes. Luge and skeleton athletes ride a flat sled.

135 MPH (217 KPH)

AVERAGE BOBSLEIGH SPEED!

LUGE

Luge riders go feet first.

brake person

pushers

BOBSLEIGH

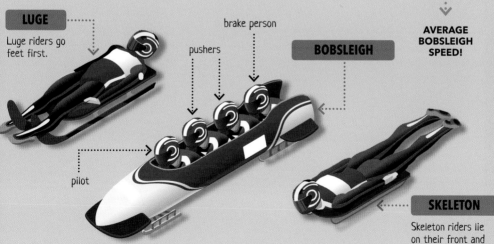

pilot

SKELETON

Skeleton riders lie on their front and travel face first!

GO QUIZ YOURSELF!

35 What is freestyle skiing and snowboarding?

36 What are three skiing disciplines?

37 What is Nordic combined?

38 How long was Stefan Kraft's 2017 world record ski jump?

39 How deep is the snowboarding halfpipe?

40 How many World Cup halfpipe wins has Chloe Kim had?

41 How many sports will feature at the Winter Olympics in 2022?

42 What is the snowboarding Big Air event?

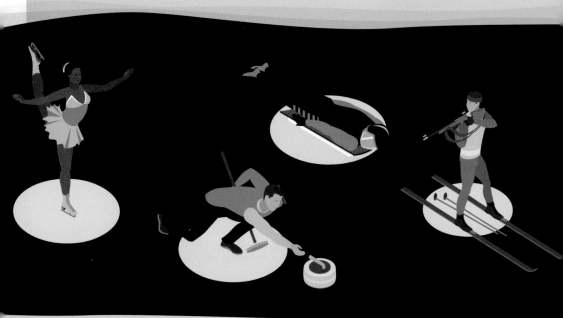

→ **43** How often do the Winter Olympics take place?

44 What is an ice hockey puck made from?

45 Name three pieces of protection that ice hockey goalies wear.

46 What distance does a long speed-skating track cover?

47 What are figure skaters judged on?

48 What are curling stones made from?

49 In curling, how many stones are used in each round?

50 On average, how fast can a bobsleigh travel?

51 How do luge athletes ride the flat sled?

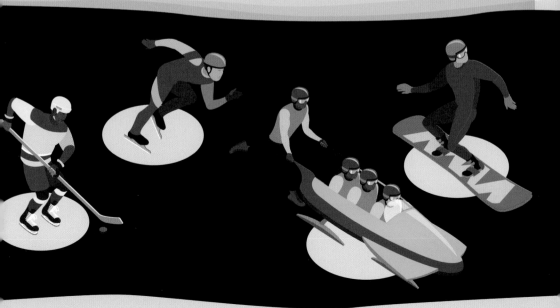

BAT AND BALL

Stick and ball games have been played all over the world since the 11th century. Here are some of the most popular today!

BASEBALL

In each of nine innings, baseball teams take turns to bat and field. The batting team hits and makes runs until three players are out, then the teams switch. The team with the most runs wins.

Home runs are scored when the batter hits the ball and is able to run around all the bases at one time.

BABE RUTH, USA

2,503 games played

714 home runs scored

US $5,640,000
One of Babe Ruth's New York Yankees jerseys sold for this record amount at an **auction** in 2019!

CRICKET

Cricket is all about the wickets! Bowlers must try to knock the bales off the stumps. The batters must protect the wicket, but also score as many runs as possible. If the wicket falls, the batter is out!

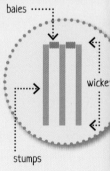

bales

wicke

stumps

out!

 Sachin Tendulkar, India

34,357 runs scored in

664 international matches

17 years old—first **Test century**

GOLF

Players use different clubs to hit a small, hard ball along the course and into a hole—in the fewest number of strokes possible. Courses usually have either 9 or 18 holes.

ADDRESS | BACKSWING | TOP BACKSWING | DOWNSWING | CONTACT | FOLLOW THROUGH

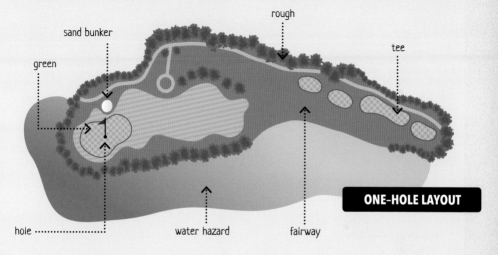

rough

sand bunker

tee

green

hole

water hazard

fairway

ONE-HOLE LAYOUT

TABLE TENNIS

Watch the ball! It's small and light, and so are the paddles that you hit it with. Matches are played individually or as doubles. Players compete for the best of five, seven, or nine games. Games are won by reaching 11 points with a clear two-point margin.

Miu Hirano and Mima Ito, Japan **14 YEARS OLD** Youngest women's doubles ITTF World Tour Grand Finals champions, 2014

BOUNCE AND TWIST

Gymnastics is just jumping and twirling, right? Wrong!
Gymnastics requires skill, stamina, flexibility**, and power!**

TYPES OF GYMNASTICS

In artistic gymnastics, athletes compete on equipment, such as vaults and bars. In rhythmic gymnastics, athletes perform routines to music using a ball, hoop, ribbon, or clubs. Acrobatics involves complex floor routines and acrobatic gymnasts perform high-energy routines to up-tempo music.

POMMEL HORSE

BEAM

FLOOR

HIGH BAR

PARALLEL BARS

PERFECT 10

In gymnastics, points are given for difficulty and execution. In 1976, Romanian gymnast Nadia Comăneci achieved the first perfect 10 in Olympic history for her uneven bars routine!

GYMNAST STARS!

 KŌHEI UCHIMURA, JAPAN

★ **3** Olympic golds
★ **10** World Championship gold medals

 SIMONE BILES, USA

★ **4** Olympic gold medals
★ **19** World Championship gold medals—the most in history
★ **25** World Championship medals—the most of any gymnast
★ **1st** female African American **all-around** World Champion

TRAMPOLINING

Boing! Boing! Trampolining routines consist of 10 moves performed one after the other. Athletes must finish their routine on their feet on the trampoline. They compete individually or in pairs. Gymnasts can reach heights of 33 feet (10 m), while performing somersaults and twists!

33 FEET (10 M)

that's the height of three African elephants!

SYNCHRONIZED SWIMMING

Pairs or teams of up to eight swimmers perform a routine of **simultaneous** moves to music. They make incredible patterns in the water, even performing lifts and jumps where some of the team will boost another out of the water!

SYNCHRO MOVES

complex patterns

lifts

elegant positions

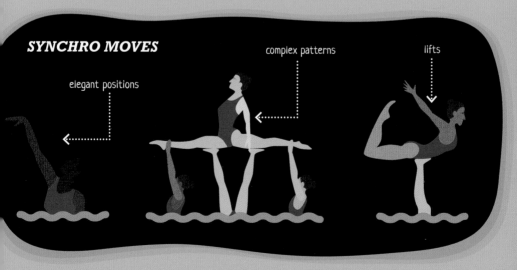

GO QUIZ YOURSELF!

52 In baseball, what is a home run?

53 How many games did baseball legend Babe Ruth play?

54 What is the role of the bowler in cricket?

55 Which country is cricketer Sachin Tendulkar from?

56 How old was Sachin Tendulkar when he scored his first Test century?

57 How many holes does a golf course have?

58 Name three physical features of a golf course.

59 What is a golf ball like?

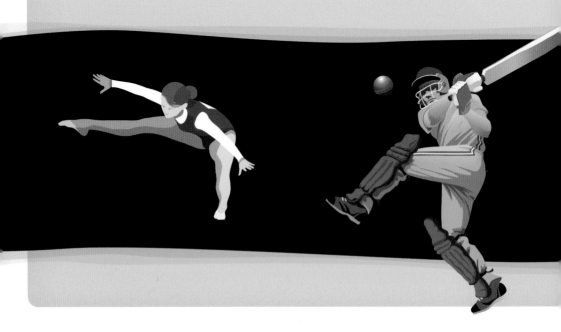

60 What points total must you reach to win a game in table tennis?

61 What age were table-tennis players Miu Hirano and Mima Ito when they won the women's doubles ITTF World Tour Grand Finals?

62 What equipment is used in rhythmic gymnastics?

63 What type of gymnastics takes place to up-tempo music?

64 Who was the first gymnast to score a perfect 10 in an Olympic competition?

65 How many Olympic gold medals does Simone Biles have?

66 How many moves make up a trampolining routine?

67 What height can trampolining gymnasts reach?

68 How many swimmers are usually in a synchronized swimming team?

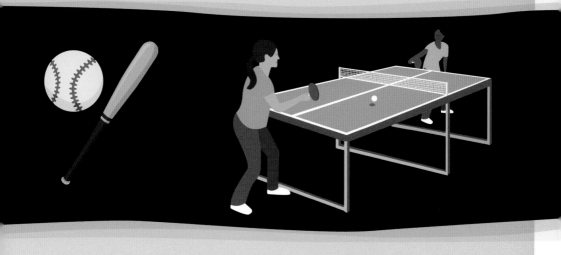

PEDAL POWER

It's time to jump on your bike and get pedaling. Professional cycling takes incredible fitness and athletic ability. Races call for stamina and careful tactics!

ROAD RACING

The first city-to-city road race took place between Paris and Rouen, France, in 1869. Today, these races are popular all over the world, with the top cyclists taking on the Grand Tours. One of the most famous is the Tour de France. The other two Grand Tours are the Giro d'Italia and the Vuelta a España.

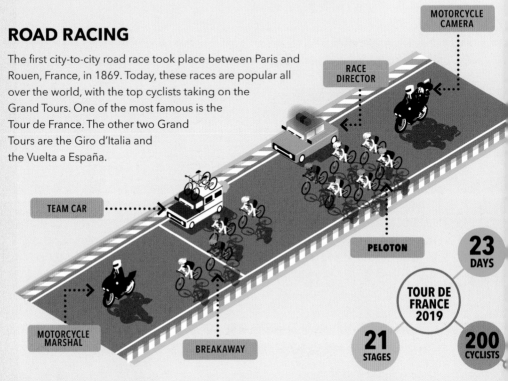

MOTORCYCLE CAMERA

RACE DIRECTOR

TEAM CAR

PELOTON

MOTORCYCLE MARSHAL

BREAKAWAY

23 DAYS

TOUR DE FRANCE 2019

21 STAGES

200 CYCLISTS

TRACK CYCLING

Track cycling takes place inside a velodrome on a track with curves that tilt at 45 degrees. Riders race around the lowest level of the track, using the slopes to overtake competitors or switch places with teammates. Track cyclists use fixed-gear bikes with no brakes!

DAME SARAH STOREY, GREAT BRITAIN

Sarah Storey gained 5 gold Paralympic swimming medals before switching to cycling. She has 9 gold Paralympics cycling medals and 31 World Championship medals. As well as competing in para events, Sarah also competes against able-bodied athletes.

MOUNTAIN BIKE

This daredevil sport has four specialties: cross-country, marathon, downhill, and four-cross. Each takes place on a course of natural obstacles, mud, rocks, dips, bumps, and bends!

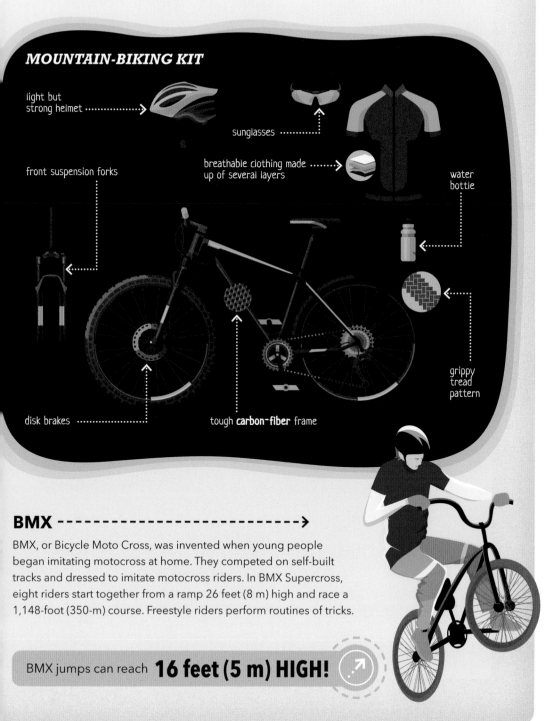

MOUNTAIN-BIKING KIT

light but strong helmet

sunglasses

front suspension forks

breathable clothing made up of several layers

water bottle

grippy tread pattern

disk brakes

tough **carbon-fiber** frame

BMX

BMX, or Bicycle Moto Cross, was invented when young people began imitating motocross at home. They competed on self-built tracks and dressed to imitate motocross riders. In BMX Supercross, eight riders start together from a ramp 26 feet (8 m) high and race a 1,148-foot (350-m) course. Freestyle riders perform routines of tricks.

BMX jumps can reach **16 feet (5 m) HIGH!**

RIDING HIGH

A strong bond is essential for equestrian sports. Each athlete is part of a partnership because rider and horse are judged together. The rider must communicate with reins, legs, and bodyweight.

REIN IT IN

Equestrian events include dressage, where the rider leads the horse through a precise series of moves; and show jumping, where the team completes a course of show jumps up to 6.6 feet (2 m) high. Eventing competitions take place over several days and include dressage, jumping, and a 3.7-mile (6-km) cross-country course with fences and jumps.

rails

HOORAY FOR HALLA

At the 1956 Olympics, rider Hans Günter Winkler was injured but wanted to finish the competition. He managed to mount his horse, Halla, but could not give her any direction. She completed the course without fault, and they won individual and team gold medals!

26!

Germany has won the most Olympic gold equestrian medals.

water jump

double bars

POLO

Teams of mounted riders compete to score the most goals. Games are divided into "chukkas"—sessions of seven minutes each. Players switch to fresh ponies in the intervals and, at half time, the spectators are invited onto the pitch to stamp down the **divots**!

POLO'S PRINCE

Adolfo Cambiaso has held the number one spot in polo rankings for an incredible 22 years! At 19 years old, he was the youngest player to reach the 10-goal handicap—the highest possible in the sport. Added to this, he's won a total of 164 titles!

Bathtime! Top polo horses have therapy baths to look after their muscles.

wall

triple bars

THWACK!

Polo players use long-handled clubs to strike the ball.

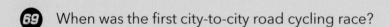

GO QUIZ YOURSELF!

69 When was the first city-to-city road cycling race?

70 Aside from the Tour de France, name the other two Grand Tours.

71 How many stages made up the 2019 Tour de France?

72 What is special about track-cycling bikes?

73 What sport did Dame Sarah Storey compete in before cycling?

74 Name two mountain biking specialities.

75 What material can mountain-bike frames be made from?

76 How high is the start ramp for BMX Supercross?

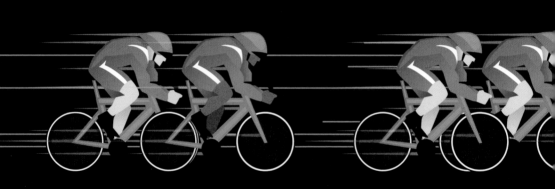

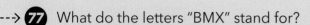

77 What do the letters "BMX" stand for?

78 Name three equestrian events.

79 How long is an equestrian cross-country course?

80 Which country has won more Olympic gold equestrian medals than any other?

81 How high are the jumps in a show-jumping ring?

82 At which Olympics were Hans Günter Winkler and Halla a winning team?

83 In polo, what are the play sessions called?

84 What do players do at the intervals in a polo match?

85 How many titles has polo player Adolfo Cambiaso won?

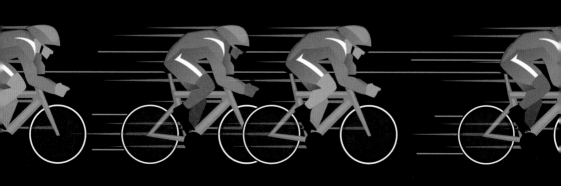

TAKE THAT!

Many combat sports have their roots in martial arts or in ancient wrestling.

JUDO

Judo was adapted from "jujitsu"—a traditional Japanese martial art. "Judo" means "the gentle way." Students learn physical elements, controls, throws, and kicks, as well as the judo moral code.

KARATE

Karate participants are called karateka. There are two elements: kata and kumite. Kata are set movements that are practiced and performed by individuals. Kumite means sparring or fighting.

98
kata to choose from!

WHAT TO WEAR

Judo and karate participants wear loose white trousers and a coat fastened with a belt. The color of the belt depends on the athlete's level of training.

Karate-gi or judo-gi (*gi* means "uniform")

belt or *obi*

WRESTLING

Greco-Roman wrestlers can use only the top half of their body; freestyle wrestlers can use any part. To win a **bout**, one opponent must pin the other to the mat for two seconds. Points can also be gained for holds during the bout.

ATCHOO!

All wrestlers must carry a white handkerchief. Failing to carry one results in a warning!

BOXING

Boxers compete in a square-shaped ring. The aim is to strike your opponent above the waist to score points or knock your opponent down for 10 seconds to win. A bell sounds to signal the end of each round.

MUHAMMAD ALI

Born Cassius Clay, Ali was–in his own words–the greatest!

★ **3** times World Heavyweight Champion

★ won **56** out of **61** professional bouts

★ **31** fights in a winning streak

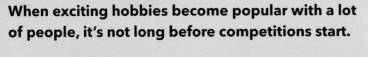

FAR OUT

When exciting hobbies become popular with a lot of people, it's not long before competitions start.

SURFING

Surfing is thought to have originated with ancient Polynesian cultures. It gained popularity in the 1960s and the first World Championship was held in 1964. There are many types of boards, but only shortboards are used in the Olympics.

SHORTBOARD pointed tip, 5.9 feet (1.8 m) long

LONGBOARD rounded tip, 8.9 feet (2.7 m) long

WINDSURFING

This exciting sport uses wind rather than wave power. Windsurfers control the craft by changing the sail position. Competitions include races and freestyle events in which contestants perform aerial tricks!

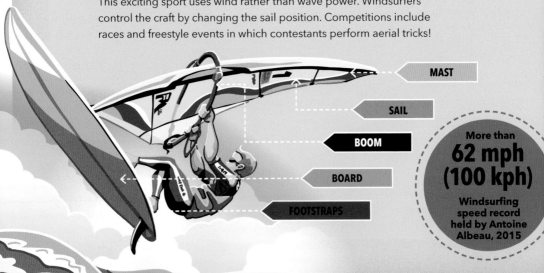

MAST

SAIL

BOOM

BOARD

FOOTSTRAPS

More than
**62 mph
(100 kph)**
Windsurfing speed record held by Antoine Albeau, 2015

CLIMBING

Rock climbers scramble over boulders or up steep cliff faces. Sport climbing was to have been included for the first time at the 2020 Olympic Games. This takes place on an indoor climbing wall and includes bouldering, speed, and lead climbing. In speed climbing, contestants compete for the fastest time up a 49-foot (15-m) wall. Freeclimbers scale incredible heights with no ropes or other equipment.

EL CAPITAN
▼

Alex Honnold freeclimbed almost 3,000 feet (914 m) up El Capitan in Yosemite National Park, USA.

El Capitan is more than three times the height of the **Eiffel Tower!**

Alex also climbed El Capitan route The Nose in record time **1hr 58 minutes.**

SKATEBOARDING

Following the rise in wave surfing, "sidewalk surfing" began. People made their own skateboards from shaped wooden boards and roller skate wheels!

TONY'S TIMELINE!

Legendary skater Tony Hawk started young and made it big. He went on to win 11 World Championships in a row!

1968
Tony was born

1977
9 years old: given first skateboard

1982
14 years old: started pro skating

1984
16 years old: best skater in the world!

GO QUIZ YOURSELF!

86 What does "judo" mean?

87 Along with the physical elements, what do judo students learn?

88 What is the belt called in a judo or karate uniform?

89 How long must a boxer's opponent be down in order for them to win?

90 How many fights did boxer Muhammad Ali win in a row?

91 What are karate participants called?

92 What is karate sparring called?

93 What are the main two types of wrestling?

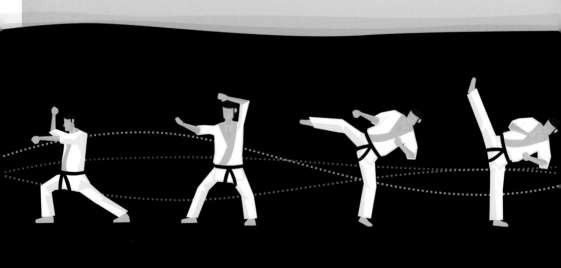

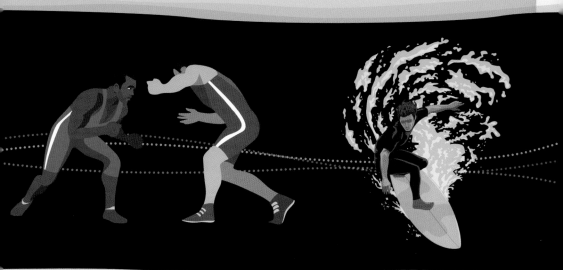

UNUSUAL SPORTS

BASE jumping, horseball, zorbing, kite skiing, sandboarding, and underwater football are all new sports. Here are some more unusual sports!

SUMO WRESTLING

In Japan's national sport, competitors attempt to push each other out of a ring. Heavyweight competitors weigh more than 330 pounds (150 kg)—about the same as a giant panda!

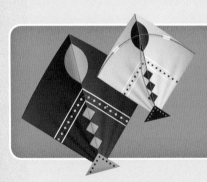

KITE FIGHTING

A professional sport in Thailand, the all-Thailand championships are held in spring every year. In kite fighting competitions, competitors battle to bring down each other's kites!

DRAGON BOAT RACING

This 2,000-year-old sport began in China. Dragon boats have the head and tail of the dragon carved at the front and back. Rowers use oars with a claw design and a drummer rides in the boat, too!

NO MORE CROQUET!

Just as sports are added to the Olympics, others are taken away. The following are no longer part of the games: rope climb, tug-of-war, distance plunging, live pigeon shooting, croquet, roque, duelling pistols, and horse long jump.

1ST PLACE

Never mind the gold medals or tall trophies, some tournaments have more interesting prizes!

CHEESE

(a 9-lb (4-kg) wheel of double Gloucester)—Coopers Hill Cheese Rolling, England

A COW

Alpine ski races

A GRANDFATHER CLOCK

NASCAR races in Martinsville, Virginia

MILK

Indianapolis 500—competitors specify milk type preference before they start!

A POLKA-DOT JERSEY

King of the Mountains in the Tour de France—awarded to the rider who scores the most points on the Tour's many climbs.

QUIZ TIME!

When you've finished testing yourself, why not use this book to make a quiz to test your friends and family? You could take questions from each section to make different rounds, or mix and match across the book for a general knowledge sports quiz. You can even make up your own quiz questions! Use these strange sports facts to get you started. For example, **"Where did Dragon Boat racing originate?"** or **"Name a sport no longer in the Olympics."**

ANSWERS

1. Keep healthy, stay active, and have fun
2. 8,000 sports worldwide
3. Wrestling
4. Volleyball, soccer, gymnastics, and capoeira
5. 8 gold medals
6. Hands and forearms
7. 169 goals
8. 10 yards (30 feet /9 m)
9. 35 goals
10. League and Union
11. 148 caps
12. 3 seconds
13. 24 seconds
14. 3 hits
15. Snow
16. Nicolas Mahut and John Isner
17. 163.7 mph (263.4 kph)
18. Long jump, triple jump, high jump, pole vault
19. 10 events
20. Track event
21. 400 m
22. More than 300 events
23. Tokyo, Japan
24. 22 sports
25. 7 events
26. Front crawl, backstroke, breaststroke, or butterfly
27. 12 gold medals
28. Platforms are higher
29. 16 feet (5 m)
30. An offshore race with a distance greater than 800 miles (1,287 km)
31. 16 years old
32. 210 days

33. One oar each
34. 9 World Championship gold medals
35. An event in which athletes complete aerial moves and tricks
36. Alpine, ski jumping, and cross-country
37. Combined cross-country skiing and ski jumping
38. 831.7 feet (253.5 m)
39. 22 feet (6.7 m)
40. 5 World Cup halfpipe wins
41. 7 winter sports
42. Performing snowboard aerial tricks from a ramp 161 feet (49 m) high
43. Every 4 years
44. Hard rubber
45. Helmet, gloves, leg pads, arm/chest protector, or blocker
46. 1,312 feet (400 m)
47. Execution and accuracy
48. Polished granite
49. 8 stones per round
50. 135 mph (217 kph)
51. On their backs, feet first
52. When a player hits the ball and is able to run around all the bases at one time
53. 2,503
54. To knock the bales off the stumps
55. India
56. 17 years old
57. 9 or 18 holes
58. Tee, fairway, rough, water hazard, sand bunker, green, or hole
59. Small and hard
60. 11 points
61. 14 years old
62. Ball, ribbon, hoop, and clubs

63 Acrobatic gymnastic floor routines

64 Nadia Comăneci scored a perfect 10

65 4 Olympic gold medals

66 10 moves

67 33 feet (10 m)

68 Up to 8 swimmers

69 1869

70 Giro d'Italia, Vueleta a España

71 21 stages

72 They have fixed gears and no brakes

73 Paralympic swimming

74 Cross-country, marathon, downhill, or four-cross

75 Carbon fiber

76 26 feet (8 m) high

77 Bicycle Moto Cross (X)

78 Dressage, show jumping, eventing

79 3.7 miles (6 km) long

80 Germany

81 Up to 6.6 feet (2 m) high

82 1956 Olympics

83 Chukkas

84 Switch to fresh ponies

85 164 titles

86 The gentle way

87 The judo moral code

88 An obi

89 10 seconds

90 31 fights in a row

91 Karateka

92 Kumite

93 Greco-Roman and freestyle

94 A white handkerchief

95 1964

96 8.9 feet (2.7 m) long

97 By changing the sail position

98 Antoine Albeau holds the speed record

99 Climbers compete for the fastest time up a 49-foot (15-m) wall

100 Climbing without ropes or other equipment

101 Sidewalk surfing

102 16 years old

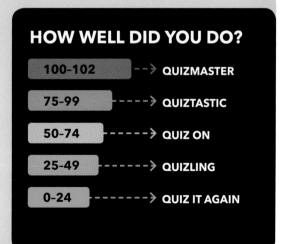

HOW WELL DID YOU DO?

100–102 --→ QUIZMASTER

75–99 -----→ QUIZTASTIC

50–74 ------→ QUIZ ON

25–49 -------→ QUIZLING

0–24 --------→ QUIZ IT AGAIN

GLOSSARY

aerial Something that happens in the air

all-around In gymnastics, describing a competition where athletes compete on all pieces of equipment

auction A sale of items where people offer money and the item is sold to the highest bidder

bout A wrestling or boxing match

cap A player's appearance in a game at an international level

carbon fiber A thin, strong material made from the natural element carbon

century In cricket, a score of 100 runs

conceded Failed to stop a goal from being scored against you

disciplines Activities that require training

divot A piece of turf cut out of the ground by the strike of a polo or golf club

dominate To be more powerful than your competition

execution The technique or style with which a person performs an act or movement

FIFA The Fédération Internationale de Football Association, which is the international governing body of soccer

flexibility The ability to move one's joints easily

granite A hard type of rock

marathon A distance running race of 26.219 miles (42.195 km)

martial art System of self-defense or attack developed from practices used by soldiers in Japan, China, and Korea

medley A swimming race in which swimmers use different strokes

nautical miles A measurement of distance at sea, 6,076 feet (1,852 m)

Nordic Relating to Scandinavian countries, Norway, Sweden, Finland, and Iceland

peloton The main group of cyclists in a race

precision Exact and accurate

rally In a racket sport: a set of back-and-forth shots between players

simultaneous Done at the same time

slalom A winding downhill skiing course marked by poles

somersaults To turn head over heels in the air or on the ground

stamina The ability to keep going for a long time

Test A cricket match played by national representative teams that takes place over a period of up to five days

FURTHER INFORMATION

BOOKS

Buckley Jr, James. *Year in Sports 2020*. Scholastic, 2019.

Ignotofsky, Rachel. *Women in Sport: 50 Fearless Athletes Who Played to win*. Wren & Rook, 2018.

Mason, Paul. *The Unofficial Guide to Olympic Events/Champions*. Wayland, 2020.

Nuñez, Jhonny. *The Ancient Olympic Games*. Wayland, 2019.

Zweig, Eric. *Everything Sports: All the Photos, Facts, and Fun to Make You Jump!* National Geographic Kids, 2016.

WEBSITES

www.olympic.org
The webpage of the Olympic Games gives information on Summer, Winter, and Youth Games, along with results, history, athletes, and more!

www.paralympic.org
The website of the Paralympic movement gives information on the athletes to watch, Paralympic sports, and classifications.

https://gaisf.sport
The GAISF oversees all sports federations. Look here for links to member federations and information on the World Urban and Combat Games.

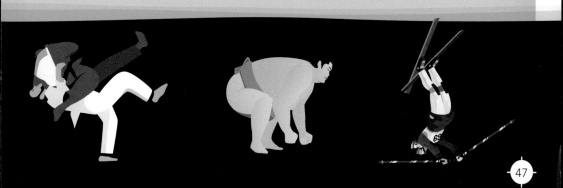

INDEX